SEVENTEEN ODES

Patrick White

Acknowledgements: *Poetry (Chicago), Prism International, Sparks, Literature Today, Anthology of Magazine Verse & Yearbook of American Poetry, 1980, Sasquatch, Dalhousie Review,* CKCU-FM, Ottawa.

Published by Fiddlehead Poetry Books, Fredericton, N.B., 1982, with the assistance of the University of New Brunswick and The Canada Council.

© Patrick White, 1982

Cover design by Alex McGibbon

Cataloguing in Publication Data

White, Patrick, 1948-
   Seventeen odes

ISBN 0-86492-014-8

I. Title.

PS8595.H57S48   C811'.54   C82-094890-X
PR9199.3.W518S48

CONTENTS

The Art of Island Gulls
The End of Labouring
The Gesture
After Completing a Long Poem, Nov. 6, 1975
An Ode: To John Keats
Shaula is the Name of the Star at the End
From a Photograph of My Wife
In Pursuit of an Earthly Excellence
Mars
Ouideis
Lyre
The Legend in Andromeda
Rags of April's Finery
For My Daughter
The Revision
Backyard Roses
Below the Salt

— for Michael R. Best,
friend and teacher

THE ART OF ISLAND GULLS

Like figure-skaters testing uncut ice,
Seagulls span their wings and ride a breeze
As cold and clean as silver blades that slice
A Russian dancer through a turn with such amazing ease
Science that has laboured into art
Would rinse the sceptic from his tampered tears.
A rink, a piece of paper, or the sky,
So many things grow relative with years;
Fool or sage, the generalizing heart
Engraves a locket for its counterpart.
Poet, skater, bird; what trinities am I?

Disciplines are attributes of energy.
A way is found to cleave the hardest gem;
An eye performing crystal surgery
Lets its charge suggest a stratagem;
A compromise is struck, the gleaming plane
Is skater's edge, or poet's mirror line,
A wing more sensitive than lover's comb
Parting tangled hair sweet vagrancies entwine.
What dance is locked within that frozen pane,
What flight, the air; through wild terrain
What river guides the poet home?

I watch the gulls negotiate their chance;
They rise, then stall, then tilt their wings to sweep
Like sabers thrilled to signal some advance
When tactics win advantage from the steep.
Aloft, their genius must first comply
With any hazard of the teeming air
They feel upon their wings; adjustments made,
I watch them sleight exquisite curves that veer
Through space as if perfection would belie
The very element instructing it to fly.
Their ultimate realities? Science and charade.

THE END OF LABOURING

Orange leaves against a mouse-grey sky;
Spiders sulk in corner windowpanes
Or spin a silken bobbin round a fly.
Everything is wet; cold November rains
Drip from cables high above the street
Where crows harass a clumsy gull
For pickings off a compost-heap.
The moon has phased three-quarters full,
And plenty's horn is left a broken hull
When autumn tides and human spirits neap.
All night the tomcats howl in heat.

Why, when life seems most about to yield
A hard-won harvest to the tenant-heart
That worked from wilderness its ample field,
Does death then take straw effigies apart
As if a vagrant sizing up a suit
Not worn out at knees, and stands in stead
Of those poor wardens even sparrows mocked?
Now all the summer's birds have fled
And mice that nested in those sleeves are dead.
Heart laboured on, till death unfrocked
A counterpart, and struck its harvest to the root.

Winter clouds could not be burdened more
Than is the heart with harm of giving up
Its crucial acreage. Too high a store
Was set upon this autumn's wasted crop.
Though heart may tend, and what is sown
Thrive well in slow-maturing soil,
Death will have the major benefit.
The end of labouring, the end of toil
Comes to nothing but this meagre spoil.
Heart must learn to glean its little bit
With winter wrens, accept its small renown.

THE GESTURE

Strange cuneiform, these bird tracks in the snow.
I read the message on my window ledge
And think how winter treats the sparrow
Who's taken shelter in the cedar hedge.
He and all his nervous company
Can only know the hunger and the death
That lingers with this blue transforming snow.
The god descends in clouds of human breath
And from a breadbox flings a spree
Of crusts and crumbs as if a yearly fee
For some small service rendered long ago.

I've spread the bounty which is waste to me
And sit behind a foggy windowpane
To watch them test my brief divinity.
The snow is blonde with summer's precious grain.
One, the leader, or the hungriest,
Perches in an apple-tree, then flutters down;
A track of tiny tridents mark the snow.
A cloud of powder, brilliant thistledown,
Is shaken from the upper boughs by all the rest
Who wait to see if anything molest
The scout who dares the perils down below.

The gestures of a god are serious
To such as these; though gods enjoy this game
Of hide and seek, or simply curious,
A kindness done for neither praise nor blame,
Wait to see the outcome of their deed;
These must risk their lives in earnest for a crumb.
Having weighed my slight munificence,
Two by two, they warily succumb.
I note the fierce intensity with which they feed,
And see in them the makings of a creed
Who'd greet my gesture, Great Significance.

AFTER COMPLETING A LONG POEM, NOV. 6, 1975

Thunder salvoes its blank batteries
Above October hills. What battle's won
Or lost? What widows made? What ease
Is shaken by the sudden thunder of a gun?
Lightning flutters on the leafless apple-trees
Mimicing its brief divinity. Heart
Be still; you tremble like a rabbit in a hutch;
Is noise alone enough to make you start
And flashbulb lightning strike you to your knees?
That work is done; and all our obsequies.
Stand up! There is no courage in a crutch.

What heartwood does the lightning seek?
A storm is passing like a manta ray
Above our heads. Will we be numbered with the meek
Who in the shadow if its wings have learned to pray?
What verdict is a shock? What judge, a tail
So arbitrary that it seems mere chance
Lightning draws you from its lottery?
Heart, we must teach fear to dance
When thunder turns our eagles into quail.
Such abuse preambles only hail;
Our hunters' shot will melt like mockery.

Then down it comes, assaulting windowpanes,
And the wings of more determined birds than those
Who shelter in the trees, poor weathervanes
Who fear to fly against a wind that blows
Them far off course. Find no fault, my heart,
With their safe estimates; they may prove wiser yet.
But brace yourself to span this turbulence
With stronger wings than is appropriate
For lesser flight. We fly without a chart,
And take against the storm, our own part.
So islanders have sometimes come to continents.

AN ODE: TO JOHN KEATS

One and one half centuries you've lain in your grave;
Life, at twenty-five, impossible to bear.
Have you any notion what you gave
So many minds? I hope somehow you are aware
Your 'genius-loving heart' still glows
A ripened coal upon that iron grate,
The last of autumn cherishing the light
By which I read, although it's getting late,
What authors you admired, what masters chose.
Sea-winds strip the lone delinquent rose
In gardens here; November's damp with blight.

That laurel wreath that made you so ashamed
Remembering the incident, is yours.
Few, as you, would think they had profaned
To wear it. A rash upon those giaours
Who at the coronation of their Christ
Assume his thorns, and think themselves the same.
I say it for the two of us, perhaps
Remembering myself a secret claim
My ego made, good Bonapartist,
Unto itself its own apologist.
All its crowns were fashioned fools' caps.

I hope not anymore, but that's a chance
I've learned to take. Why go at all
If I object to join the dance
For fear someone might see me fall?
Your example motions me to rise
And let the music guide my fumbling feet,
And more, and so much more
I could not know by staying in my seat
While others dance despite the eyes
Muted round the room, who'd have the prize
You escorted to the open floor.

You'd glory in the sumac now, though rain
Contrives to put that phoenix out, its fire
Much like yours, the fire in the grain
Each autumn purifies upon a pyre
More splendid than the last; the rain has failed.
You fed upon the ashes of your youth
Three years, a true Shakespearean.
The heart is where we store the warm truth
You final poems are, their beauty flailed
From full experience. You have prevailed,
Most among the miracles of men, a man.

SHAULA IS THE NAME OF THE STAR AT THE END

Blue acetylene, Scorpio returns;
If stars were weeds, it would be yarrow.
Chimneys are as cold as summer urns.
What time is it?—it must be late—tomorrow
I suppose; the grass is stiff with frost.
All the planets are in view, and there,
Elusive Mercury, exquisite thrill
Of steady lilac light so rare
Staid Copernicus, condemned to roast
In hell, had given up his book and ghost
Without a glimpse of it. The air is still.

I had hoped to clear my mind of thoughts
More insistent than the summer wasps
That swarm upon decaying apricots.
I sought a coma from those regal asps,
Poetry and wine, a long retreat,
But both had lost their power to appease
My growing hate. Incited by a friend,
Betrayal summoned older treacheries
His company had helped me once unseat
And render all their bitter poison sweet.
Shaula is the name of the star at the end.

Scorpions will sting themselves to death,
Warding off the sickly smell of ants.
How did my friend disguise his breath?
Like that lilac planet that enchants
The eastern sky, he pales before the dawn;
Quicksilver courier, he welled my ears
With lies enough to kill a dozen kings.
Is there a potion in a poet's tears?
I cannot see him now; no, he's gone.
Copernicus has put him near the sun;
I still can hear the flutter of fleeing wings.

FROM A PHOTOGRAPH OF MY WIFE

This is for you whose hair is bronzed by dusk
Beneath a plum-tree's dusty summer leaf;
I have something to say you didn't have to ask
Concerning love, and us, and what can ease the grief
When there is time to think beyond today.
I have this photograph of you, your lovely hair
Long and loose and cloyed with copper light;
I have a lifetime for the woman standing there,
And though the wind blow leaf away
Or lose it to the damp asylum of the clay,
I'd set this much for us against the coming night:

There is a planet in the early western light
That monthly climbs to fall diurnally,
And when the moon is new, or out of sight,
It's one of three to cast a shadow naturally.
Hesperus or Venus, as you will,
I've watched it since a solitary boy,
First initiate to mystery,
At summer dusk, ingenuous as joy,
Would climb the broken rocks up Heartbreak Hill
To see it shining high above the paper-mill.
You've guessed, of course, that boy was me.

But there's another place that light can be,
And other things a star might mean.
It rises now before the sun can free
One sparrowful of dawn's adrenaline.
I can't recall its eastern name;
It seems enough to know it's simply there,
A symbol of the way our love has changed
From summer-night to winter-morning star.
So are and are we not perhaps the same;
But if our only option's been the picture-frame,
It's good to know the rest was somehow prearranged.

IN PURSUIT OF AN EARTHLY EXCELLENCE

The trees at night, the streetlights and the rain;
The leaves are soggier than wasted cereal.
I know the bland fulfillment of the sane;
I tinker with a fussy aerial.
My heart's been wheeled away, an invalid;
I can no more than guess at what is wrong.
I wished the worst be done that it might pass,
But being done, there ended days of song.
I loathe my lot. Who'll open with a bid?
An auctioneer has certified me dead.
I gorge the gullet of an hourglass.

Satisfied? Content? What song can come of that?
I do not think a robin sings to please:
He sings because he's twice escaped the cat.
The spring is full of high-pitched victories.
An adversary gives him cause to sing,
And singing is an earthly excellence;
A song is drowned with any bag of cats.
The dead alone leave nothing out for chance;
All the reckless robins come the spring
Will celebrate the risks of wintering
While caution stammers with its diplomats.

An auctioneer, an hourglass, a bird:
Three throats are full of my predicament.
Something counsels me to pick the third;
The other two can claim whatever rent
They feel is due: I slam the door. I quit.
November's ruin is delight to me—
God hang goiters from their ugly throats;
I denounce their weak conformity—
Or catch them passing shoddy counterfeit.
My heart returns, joy's misfit.
These squandered leaves are promissory notes.

MARS

A 'seeing night' astronomers would say,
No moon, no mist, a cold tranquillity.
Mars now makes its slow triumphant way
Above the trees, their colours struck, a fee
Of oaks, leaf-legions dead upon the field;
Mars now strides through ruin and defeat.
Bright minister of war, red ant,
Are you assured your carnage is complete?
I recognize those faces on your shield;
Before you, even love must yield:
Your tactic? Feigned retreat. Your orbit? Aberrant.

You double back, a tiger on its spoor,
Your unsuspecting hunters now the prey.
Their dogs are frenzied by the warm allure
Of cunning bait. Your killing's play,
And men no less than dogs are savaged so.
I see you through bare branches now, alone;
Napoleon reviewing Austerlitz,
Alaric reeling through the streets of Rome.
Wherever men have been, there is that glow;
Indian jungle or Siberian snow—
Your light recoils through evil transits.

You billet fear in all our dwellings;
We bar the doors, and board the windows up.
Fear has lodged with softer finer feelings
Than ever served its bitter cup;
Your agents riot in our daughters' hair;
Suspicion stamps the heart's expired pass;
You stock our silos with contaminated grain;
And yet, and yet, you are an alias,
Bright assumption of an arid star,
Your moons race round you, the tortoise and the hare,
Demos, Phobos: illusions hunters feign.

OUDEIS

What would rage demand? A servitude?
Three hundred years the eye of Jupiter,
A rabbit-pink, enflamed by some unknown feud,
Has raged like that duped monitor
The Greeks put out. A lethal hurricane,
Will no one spare an eye to obviate
The cruel weather of this sightless king?
What worlds might salvaged irises donate?
Would Jupiter awake, and kings be kings again,
Would boys and lovers, that majestic train
Of duckling moons; would they reflower spring?

We can be punished for a thousand things
And still not know the sly tormentor's name
We'd castigate for all our sufferings
When others ask where we would fix the blame.
A patch is put upon a ruptured eye;
I think of Milton writing in eclipse—
Are wife and daughters those attending moons
I see tonight? What dark apocalypse
Do they transcribe, what infernal alibi
Must rage usurp their souls to justify?
I think of butterflies in grey cocoons.

Are angels hurled like rocks from heaven's cliff,
And gardens locked behind a man and wife,
And do her features harden to a hieroglyph
When nervous fingers read that tale of strife,
Because Nobody cauterized an eye?
Rage grows strict when centuries prolong
Its pain; it masters vision's underlings
And bids them serve the strange polemic of its song,
Its pain asylums summer's butterfly;
But sight restored, how could it justify
That thrall of moons, of women, or of wings?

LYRE

The birch-tree trunks are white as plaster casts
And advokat, their leaves, a custard yellow,
Trembling in the wind, bleached enthusiasts,
While skies grow dark as overcast Othello.
A blonde and healthy girl, a soft caress,
Kind enough to love, round enough for lust,
How many years ago were we abed
That night a storm developed from a gust
And calm as salt, she started to undress,
And numb, I viewed her nakedness,
A body sweet and warm as winter bread?

And wine, the drowsy lovers must have wine
And shadows guttering with candlelight,
And take it for a most propitious sign
A moth has found a refuge from the night;
And afterglow of embering desire
Must keep a second-storey window lit,
And comfort any passerby who braves,
For reasons only he can posit,
The icy rain, and high demonic choir
That shrieks through powerlines as if a lyre
Could still be why such brutal weather waves.

I've passed that window many times since then,
Rectangle silvered by a summer moon,
Or idle musing of distracted pen
When themes and leaves and images are strewn
Along the grey abandoned avenue
Where rustling birches luminous with rain
Recall one winter's strange delirium;
I've passed, mornings on a windowpane,
As if I looked for evidence those two
Still enjoy that second-storey view,
Though lyre's tamed to tintinnabulum.

THE LEGEND IN ANDROMEDA

Two hundred million years that galaxy
Has nested on the brilliant bough
Of chained Andromeda. My infancy
Diminishing; a patch of melting snow;
I stand so far from it a billion stars
Are nothing but a smudge of smokey light.
That Whale? Its skeleton still hulls the shore;
My father left for easier excaliburs;
My mother looked in all the local bars.
I keep repeating: What's a father for?

Can anybody recollect his face?
Perseus is almost at meridian;
I constellate its stars, and try to trace
The features of what must have been a man.
Hero holds a woman's severed head,
Algol, Demon Star, Medusa, Ghoul—
Had she vipers in her hair, a living mop?
I've known too many women used like fuel,
Their warmth is life, their light is bread,
The planets sleep at the foot of their bed.
How then can her eclipse have cursed the crop?

My father rushed to rescue women on the rocks
As heroes must. Do other sons look up tonight,
Fierce brood of crippled hawks
He cast from that high nest of light?—
I too was banished from my father's eyes,
And tore at life as at my father's liver.
Hands that pitied me still bear the scars.
Now break those chains! Set free the fire-giver!
Prometheus must Perseus revise;
I come to power in forbidden skies
By rearranging all my father's stars.

RAGS OF APRIL'S FINERY

Generations waste beneath an apple-tree.
If I had known what comes with age, if love
Of anything, of art, of woman, or this tree
Had once removed the soft concealing glove
That made my love both discipline and mystery,
Would I have kissed that charge of time and death
And praised the trend of flesh's favouring?
Is there disease upon a mother's breath?—
Her lullabies were full of secrecy.
Did ruin foul the ancient nursery?
Her milk was sweet and warm, her voice, a cloak, or wing.

I love a woman and a worldly art;
My life can be consoled by shedding trees.
My youth has passed, a murmur of the heart,
And with it all my burning loyalties;
And yet, these leafless days set well with me.
I am a figure at a windowpane,
Staring at the lesson in the leaves.
The trees are dripping with a pewter rain;
A surgeon's hands are rinsed for surgery,
Children in a nurse's custody,
She fits them with miraculous reprieves.

All seasons claim the dreamer at this earthly watch.
Distractions of a dying fire, art
Hangs garments in the closet of a bitch,
At once a tailor to a virgin and a tart,
It fashions wardrobes from the fire's drapery,
Concealing which is which, divided love,
A lifelong study in a single dress,
It kisses ruin through a virgin's glove.
Those leaves are rags of April's finery;
A naked woman waits beneath the tree.
She has an ailing child and something to confess.

FOR MY DAUGHTER

The wind is whistling in the chimney-pot
As if it played upon a hollow jug.
My daughter tosses in her troubled cot.
The cat has spilled her milk and mug.
A rose-vine scratches at the windowpane;
The cat is scratching at her bedroom door.
I shoo the cat away; tie back the vine;
I mop the milk that's dribbled to the floor.
And then the wind begins to fling the rain
Against the walls and rattling windowpane:
Take all the leaves, take all; this one is mine.

No crown awaits, no fortune, nor a name;
She beat the odds against a contraceptive.
I have the chores of those who kept the flame
When neither birth nor fire were elective.
I would not have it any other way.
My daughter is a motive more than me
I do not doubt, her life is pure acclaim.
Neither love, nor art, nor death's finality
Nor anything philosophy might say
Can make me doubt this primum mobile
Who champions the little and the lame.

She inherits hate, and probably a war
To flush the future like a monthly tide.
Her life will gather to a final metaphor
Like some collapsing star whose light has sighed
And blown the tired planets out.
I will be a marker in a book
Whose labour hushed her boisterous song
And fixed her laughter with an angry look.
She, too, will know the penury of doubt
And fear the storm within as well without;
But I would have her know her birth was never wrong.

THE REVISION

How out of place, this shabby winter rose
That blooms beneath my windowpane, alone,
When mind amasses to a darker front than those
The clouds advance, burdens on a troubled bone,
An image to arrest the progress of a storm.
Why bloom at all?—bees are tucked away,
Apples gathered off the ground, and trees
Are a poison to moths that would lay
Next summer's tents, a silken swarm
Of would-be butterflies—what charm
Have you, that you've outlasted all of these?

This June, your kind had seemed to me a waste,
I thought of pampered women wilting in the heat;
Your beauty, then, was qualified by caste;
Your petals fell at anybody's feet,
But those who moved to have you for their own
You reproved with thorns. A thriving weed,
No more than what it seemed, gave me more delight.
You, conceived by luxury; it, by need;
No sight or scent of you could half atone
For hardships only stricter lives had known.
Beauty won assured me more than your birthright.

Not now; not seeing you this other way;
Petals once let fall, are less than rags;
Against the wind you wear a negligee,
And all your leaves are lost like luggage tags.
All around are weeds, wound about your throat,
And frost has hinted at the cold ordeal to come.
A poor advantage winter soon will take,
You win a dignity from martyrdom.
I now revise the last that summer wrote,
Extending this to you, a warmer coat.
You alone, of all, stayed for my sake.

BACKYARD ROSES

And still the roses bloom beside the rusty drum
Crammed with half-burnt magazines, and bills;
A symbol of our fallen state, this sum
Of beauty lingering like modern ills,
Romance and dull reality? A rose?—
How has it not been used to signify
The burdens of humanity? What man
When everything about him starts to die,
When autumn heaps the bins with summer's clothes,
Has never been associate with those
I see still thriving by an iron can?

I think of wives whose husbands overuse
The bodies they aspired to; the love
Familiarity will soon abuse.
Must phoenix then incinerate the dove,
A minor fusion of that holocaust
Whose ashes cake the starving rose?
Cold rain and fog, fog and rain,
The summer must have found a brief repose
In these, all her other features lost,
Though weather has conspired to exhaust
Her failing charms, these roses still remain.

And will remain, long after we are dust,
Our woes consolidated by a spade,
And all the lavishings of human lust
Mean nothing more than bills we haven't paid.
Generations deepen in that stain,
Altars of a troubled heart, their hue
A dark druidic smearing sacred stones.
I never could stop loving them, or you;
I will stand before you both again
In other guises, other terms of pain,
And hope somehow the sacrifice atones.

BELOW THE SALT

To hell with love, integrity, and art!—
Who'd go tuxedo to a pauper's board
And dine upon his own ungarnished heart?
My cats eat sparrows, mice, a smorgasbord
Of spiders, flies, and moths; their silverware?—
Mistress Nature sets before them teeth and claws.
I run my finger round an empty pot,
My heart again?—then where's the sauce?
Tribes have thought it much the choicest fare
When enemies were brave. Mine is rare,
Tender, hot, no bones; we've always fought.

Heat, shelter, food; where are my roses now?
Bread can bloom as well, as well entice the air;
Prefer the apple to the flower on the bough.
Let poets rave; they dress for caviare,
But Beauty seats her guests below the salt:
To her! Her health! A toast! I compliment the crust.
Holding out their bowls—is that an offering,
Or will they go for seconds on the dust?
Poverty can turn the blood to bitter malt;
Ariel to Caliban will then default
And purest notion gruel with suffering.

Hard times, my heart, hard times, old shoe;
I will not eat you yet, be still, relax
Old relish, you'd only brine the stew;
Not even autumn tries to ripen wax.
I'll call the roses back, apologize;
I'll sit with dogs, don my finest suit;
Can penguins learn to bark like pampered seals?
I know the blossom fusses for the fruit,
And Beauty has a famine in her eyes;
I will not scamp the portion she supplies;
Sometimes it's cake, sometimes these old bastilles.